T008546

Learn How to Play the Cent........... ....

ASAP

TRUMPET
METHOD

BY GERALD F. KNIPFEL

ISBN 978-1-57424-375-8
SAN 683-8022

Cover by James Creative Group
Cover Trumpet: courtesy of Conn – Selmer, Model Bach TR300H2
Special thanks to Cameron Bradley for the Trumpet Charts and music notation
Special thanks to Dan Gosling and Charles P. Conrad

Copyright © 2018 CENTERSTREAM Publishing
P.O. Box 17878 - Anaheim Hills, CA 92817

www.centerstream-usa.com | centerstrm@aol.com | 714-779-9390

All rights for publication and distribution are reserved.
No part of this book may be reproduced in any form or by any Electronic or mechanical means including information storage and
retrieval systems without permission in writing from the publisher, except by reviewers who may quote brief passages in review.

For my granddaughters,
Emily, and Julie with love

Contents

Dan Gosling

Gerry Knipfel was my primary trumpet teacher as a young student. I went on to receive degrees in trumpet performance from the University of Illinois and Northwestern University. I owe much of my college success and my 30 year career as a professional trumpet player to the fundamental lessons I learned from Gerry. And they are all here in this great new method book, including an introduction to jazz stylings!

Any young player will know they have a solid foundation by using Gerry's step-by-step approach to the trumpet. I highly recommend it!

Dan Gosling
Former member – Indianapolis Symphony Orchestra
Creator of ChopSaver Lip Care

Foreword

Gerry Knipfel was my first private trumpet teacher and my band director at Arlington High School my freshman year. He was an exemplary teacher who brought in many famous musicians to solo with the band, including the one who had the greatest impact on me as a trumpeter, the legendary Doc Severinsen. I have been a trumpeter, conductor and trumpet teacher for 42 years in Central Indiana.

This beginning trumpet book is well thought out and includes the necessary information for a successful start as a trumpeter as well as an introduction to some of the classic tunes of America, such as Grandfather's Clock, My Bonnie Lies Over the Ocean and Red River Valley. I have noticed in my own teaching that the younger students grow less aware of these historical songs every year as music courses in schools pay ever less attention to them. There are also some duets that the teacher can play with the student to help with phrasing, steady rhythm, intonation and other musical concerns. Rhythms are introduced in a manner that will help the student learn to count independently and understand the mechanics of sub-division of beats, which is a facet ignored in some beginning methods.

The Knipfel Trumpet Method is a welcome addition to the literature for beginning trumpeters, and I recommend it to trumpet teachers and band directors.

Charles P. Conrad
Music Director – Indiana Wind Symphony

Notes to the Student

✔ Do not attach the mouthpiece to the trumpet until you can get a good buzzing sound on the mouthpiece alone.

✔ The embouchure (or placement of the mouthpiece) should be approximately 1/3 upper lip and 2/3 bottom lip (1/2 and 1/2 is also possible).

✔ When blowing air through the trumpet, think about pushing it directly to the bell.

✔ Always breathe in air from the corners of your lips and never from your nose.

✔ Support the air flow with your diaphragm (tummy muscles).

✔ Keep your throat open to let air pass easily.

✔ When playing higher and louder, increase support from your diaphragm and open your throat even more.

✔ Before starting a piece of music, make a mental note of the key signature and the meter signature (find the beats!). This will help with your sight reading.

✔ Practice 30-45 minutes EVERY DAY. Remember, the more you practice, the smarter you get!

✔ Set a goal to be first chair in your ensemble.

How to Hold Your Trumpet

➥ Place your right hand thumb between the 1st and 2nd valve casings.

➥ Place the pads of your first three fingers on the tops of each valve cap.

➥ Curve your fingers in a backward "C" formation

➥ Do not place your pinky finger in the ring; place it on top.

Trumpet Fingering Chart

With only three valves, the trumpet can use a total of seven different combinations of fingers. These combinations are called "*fingerings.*"
On this page you will find a layout of many of the notes you will learn to play on the trumpet.
Lower notes are found near the bottom while higher notes are found near the top.

How does the trumpet create different notes?
The trumpet does very little of the work; YOU must help the trumpet by creating a good embouchure and using proper breath support (creating fast and steady air for the trumpet to work correctly).

How do I use this page?
When you see a circle filled in like the picture on the right, the corresponding finger must press the valve completely down (in this case your right hand's pointer finger). If the circle is empty, simply leave the pad of your fingertip resting on top of the valve without pressing down (in this case your right hand's middle and third fingers).

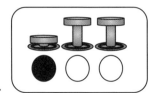

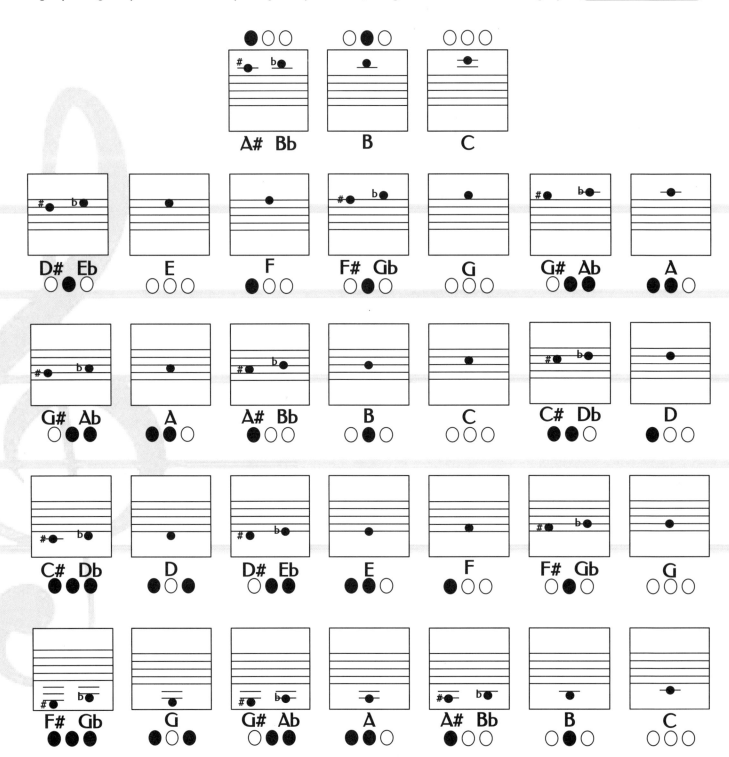

8

Advanced Trumpet Fingering Chart

A higher note that is created using the same fingering as a lower note is called a "*partial*." Try playing as many partials as you can using the columns below! Build your skills by playing left and right (changing *fingerings*) as well as up and down (changing *partials*) on this page.

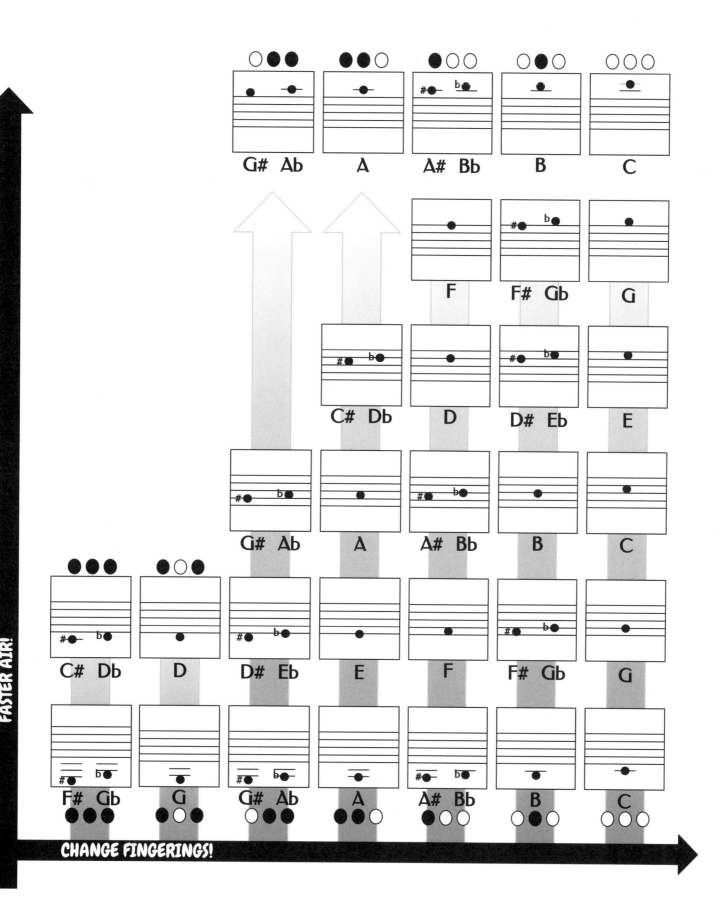

LESSON ONE

CHECK OUT THE NEW MUSICAL SYMBOLS IN EACH LESSON BEFORE MOVING ON!

LESSON TWO

COMMON TIME
EACH MEASURE GETS 4 BEATS

HALF NOTES
(COUNT 1-2)

NAME THIS SONG! "_____"

11

LESSON THREE

LESSON FOUR

NEW TIME SIGNATURE!
4- 4 BEATS PER MEASURE.
4- EACH QUARTER NOTE GETS 1 BEAT.

QUARTER NOTE
(COUNT 1)

LESSON FIVE

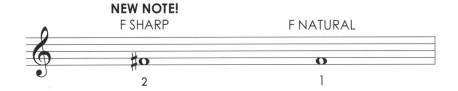

ABIDE WITH ME

14

LESSON SIX

LESSON SEVEN

NEW TIME SIGNATURE!
3- 3 BEATS PER MEASURE
4- EACH QUARTER NOTE STILL GETS ONE BEAT

QUARTER REST
(COUNT 1)

LESSON EIGHT

DON'T FORGET TO USE 2ND VALVE FOR THESE NOTES

GOODNIGHT, LADIES

LESSON NINE

LESSON TEN
LET'S REVIEW WHAT YOU KNOW!

GRANDFATHER'S CLOCK
THIS SONG BEGINS WITH "PICK-UP" EIGHTH NOTES

LESSON ELEVEN

SLURS

KEEP AIR MOVING BETWEEN NOTES,
BUT DO NOT TONGUE THE SECOND NOTE.

FOR THE BEAUTY OF THE EARTH (DUET)

LESSON TWELVE

NEW KEY SIGNATURE!

ACCENT: EMPHASIZE ANY NOTE
WITH THIS SYMBOL ATTACHED.

*DON'T FORGET TO USE 1ST VALVE
WHEN PLAYING THESE TWO NOTES.*

ABIDE WITH ME (DUET)

21

LESSON THIRTEEN

DOTTED QUARTER NOTES ARE OFTEN FOLLOWED BY A SINGLE EIGHTH NOTE

COUNT 1-2   *AND*

STARS OF THE SUMMER NIGHT

LESSON FOURTEEN

STACCATO: A DOT PLACED ABOVE OR BELOW A NOTE INDICATES
THAT A NOTE MUST BE PLAYED SHORT.

COME YE THANKFUL PEOPLE (DUET)

LESSON FIFTEEN
RITARDANDO (rit.): GRADUALLY SLOWING DOWN

THE CHALLENGE

AMERICA, MY COUNTRY (DUET)

24

LESSON SIXTEEN

NEW NOTE!
E-FLAT

NEW KEY SIGNATURE!
KEY OF B-FLAT MAJOR

REPEAT SIGN:
PLAY UNTIL THE LATTER SIGN,
THEN REPEAT BACK TO THE
FORMER AND PLAY AGAIN.

THERE'S MUSIC IN THE AIR

LESSON SEVENTEEN

DA CAPO (D.C.): "THE BEGINNING."
D.C. al fine: RETURN TO
THE BEGINNING,
THEN PLAY
UNTIL "FINE."

FINE: THE END

FERMATA:
HOLD NOTE LONGER

MY BONNIE LIES OVER THE OCEAN (DUET)

LESSON EIGHTEEN

NEW TIME SIGNATURE!
ALLA BREVE (CUT TIME):
EACH HALF NOTE NOW
RECEIVES ONE BEAT.

FIRST AND SECOND ENDINGS:
PLAY SECTION ONE,
THEN REPEAT. THEN PLAY
SECTION TWO ONLY.

RED RIVER VALLEY

LESSON NINETEEN

CUT TIME REVIEW

LESSON TWENTY

OCTAVE: THE DISTANCE BETWEEN TWO NOTES WITH THE SAME NAME.

FAMOUS MARCH STRAIN

PRACTICE: 1. REGULAR FINGERINGS
           2. 1-3 VALVES

LESSON TWENTY-ONE

CHROMATIC STUDIES

CHROMATIC:
USING EVERY HALF-STEP
IN BETWEEN ALL NOTES.

ENHARMONICS: NOTES THAT SOUND THE SAME
WITH DIFFERENT NAMES.

CHROMATIC ETUDE

LESSON TWENTY-TWO

LESSON TWENTY-THREE

LESSON TWENTY-FOUR

CHECK OUT THE NEW LENGTH OF THESE NOTE COMBINATIONS!

NEW TIME SIGNATURE!
6 BEATS PER MEASURE
EIGHTH NOTE=1 BEAT

FERMATA
(HOLD)

MY BONNIE

COUNT 1-2 + 3 4 5 6

33

LESSON TWENTY-FIVE
2 BEATS PER MEASURE

LESSON TWENTY-SIX

WHEN JOHNNY COMES MARCHING HOME

LESSON TWENTY-SEVEN

LESSON TWENTY-EIGHT

LESSON TWENTY-NINE

LESSON THIRTY

O CHRISTMAS TREE

LIP SLURS

LESSON THIRTY-ONE
SEVEN MAJOR SCALES AND ARPEGGIOS

LESSON THIRTY-TWO

CHROMATIC SCALES (THESE MAY BE PLAYED IN COMMON-TIME OR CUT-TIME)

CHROMATIC DUET

Moderato

41

LESSON THIRTY-THREE
LIP SLURS

LESSON THIRTY-FOUR
SYNCOPATION

YOU'RE A GRAND OLD FLAG (G.M. COHAN)

DOWN BY THE RIVERSIDE

LESSON THIRTY-FIVE
EIGHTH NOTES, CUT-TIME, AND SIXTEENTH NOTES REVIEW

WILLIAM TELL OVERTURE (8th Notes)

WILLIAM TELL OVERTURE (CUT-TIME)

WILLIAM TELL OVERTURE (16th Notes)

SOME JAZZ BASICS

SWINGIN' FOR TWO TRUMPETS

Rhytn Rhythms

Can you write the counts of each note and rest below?
The first line (and tips in each line) is done for you.

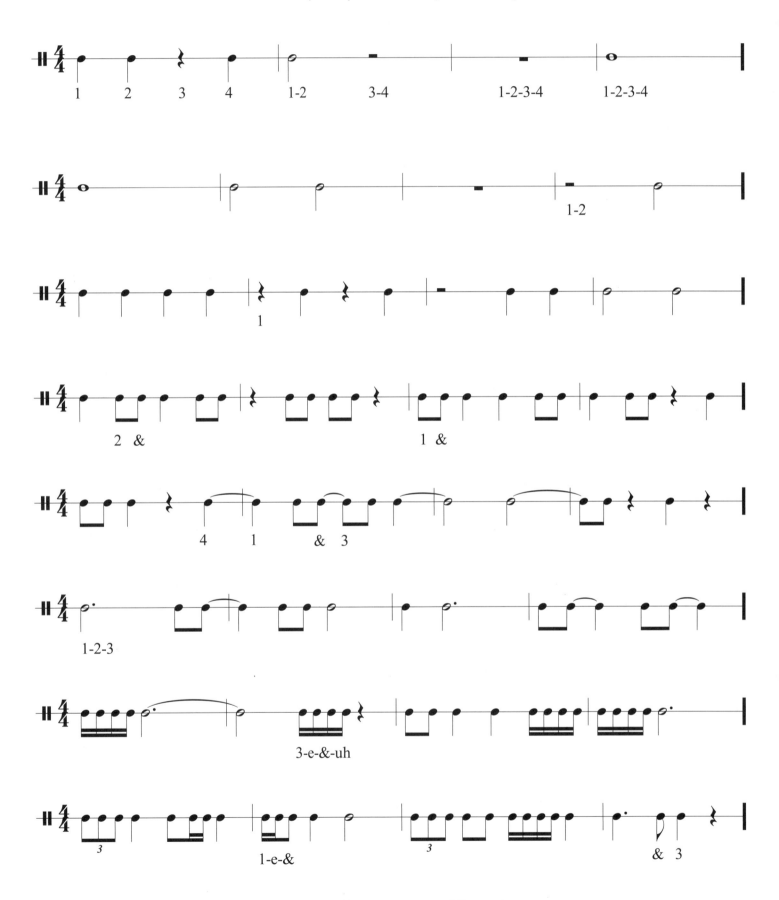

(Answers on page 51)

SYMBOLS AND TERMS

ACCENT – TO EMPHASIZE A NOTE.

AL FINE – ("AL FEE-NAY") PLAY TO THE END.

ALLA BREVE – "CUT-TIME." HALF NOTES RECEIVE ONE BEAT.

ARPEGGIO – THE NOTES WITHIN A CHORD (USUALLY NOTES 1, 3, AND 5 IN A SCALE).

CHROMATIC – USING HALF-STEPS IN BETWEEN NOTE NAMES (EX. F#). A SCALE USES ALL OF THEM.

CODA – "THE TAIL," OR A SPECIAL ENDING.

COMMON TIME – 4/4 TIME. QUARTER NOTES RECEIVE ONE BEAT.

CRESCENDO – TO GRADUALLY GET LOUDER.

CUT TIME – "ALLA BREVE." HALF NOTES RECEIVE ONE BEAT.

DA CAPO (D.C.) – THE BEGINNING. OFTEN FOUND WITH "AL FINE" (TO THE END).

DAL SEGNO (D.S.) – "THE SIGN." OFTEN FOUND WITH "AL FINE" (TO THE END) OR "AL CODA."

DECRESCENDO – TO GRADUALLY GET SOFTER. SEEN WITH SEVERAL NOTES, UNLIKE ACCENTS.

ENHARMONICS – TWO NOTES THAT SOUND THE SAME WITH DIFFERENT NAMES (EX. C# AND Db).

FERMATA – HOLD A NOTE UNTIL YOUR INSTRUCTOR INDICATES A RELEASE.

FINE – THE END.

FORTE (f) – LOUDLY.

FORTISSIMO (ff) – VERY LOUDLY.

MARCATO – A SHORT ACCENT.

MEZZO FORTE (mf) – SOMEWHAT LOUDLY.

Doc Severinsen

MEZZO PIANO (mp) – SOMEWHAT SOFTLY.

MODERATO – A MEDIUM TEMPO.

OCTAVE – DISTANCE BETWEEN TWO NOTES WITH THE SAME NAME (THE BOTTOM AND TOP OF A SCALE

PIANO (p) – SOFTLY.

RITARDANDO (rit.) – TO GRADUALLY SLOW DOWN.

SLUR – A CURVED LINE INDICATING TO NOT TONGUE TWO OR MORE DIFFERENT CONNECTED NOTES.

STACCATO – TO PLAY A NOTE SHORT.

SYNCOPATION – A STYLE OF RHYTHM THAT NATURALLY EMPHASIZES NOTES ON "AND" COUNTS.

TEMPO – THE SPEED OF THE MUSIC.

TENUTO – TO PLAY A NOTE TO ITS FULL LENGTH.

TIE – A CURVED LINE INDICATING TO NOT TONGUE TWO OR MORE OF THE SAME CONNECTED NOTES.

Rhytn Rhythms

ANSWER SHEET

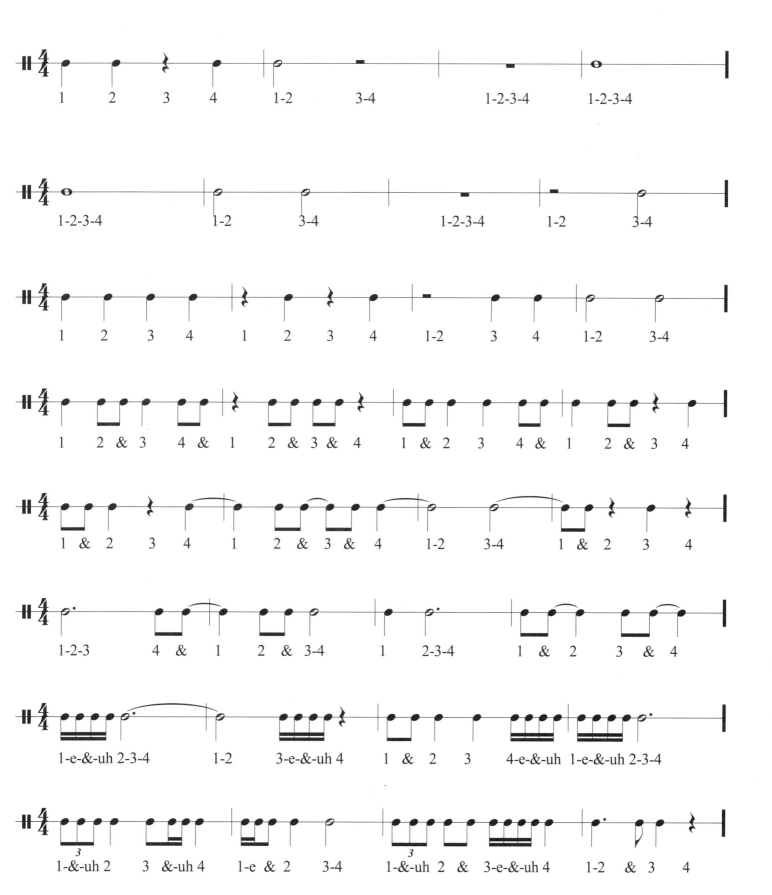

More Great ASAP Books from Centerstream...

ASAP SERIES teacher-friendly or great for self-study, these book/CD packs and DVDs will teach budding instrumentalists how to play the correct way. They're a great way to learn to play...ASAP

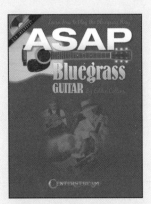

ASAP BLUEGRASS GUITAR

Learn How to Play the Bluegrass Way
by Eddie Collins
00001582 Book/2-CD Pack...........$22.99

ASAP CLASSICAL GUITAR

Learn How to Play the Classical Way
by James Douglas Esmond
00001202 Book/CD.........................$15.95

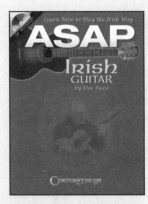

ASAP IRISH GUITAR

Learn How to Play the Irish Way
by Doc Rossi
00113683 Book/2-CD Pack............$19.99

ASAP FIDDLE TUNES MADE EASY FOR BLUEGRASS BANJO

Learn How to Play the Bluegrass Way
by Eddie Collins
00001459 Book/CD.........................$19.99

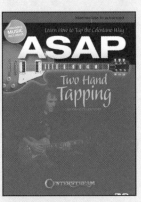

ASAP TWO-HAND TAPPING

Learn How to Play the Celentano Way
by Dave Celentano
00001292 DVD $19.99

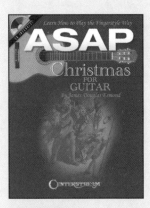

CHRISTMAS FOR GUITAR

Learn How to Play the Fingerstyle Way
by James Douglas Esmond
00001574 Book/CD Pack $14.99

You'll like what you hear!

P.O. Box 17878 - Anaheim Hills, CA 92817
(714) 779-9390   centerstrm@aol.com | www.centerstream-usa.com